Dino Tales: Loki Save the Village

First Edition: August 2024 (1.4)

ISBN 978-1-908293-64-0

Dinomedia 2024

© Peter Freeth and Emma Freeth 2024

Story: Peter Freeth, Illustration: Emma Freeth

Peter Freeth and Emma Freeth have asserted their rights under the Copyright, Designs and Patents act 1988 to be identified as the authors of this work.

All rights reserved in all media. This book may not be copied, stored, transmitted or reproduced in any format or medium without specific prior permission from the publisher.

Dinomedia is an imprint of Genius Media

Genius Media, B1502, PO Box 15113, Birmingham, B2 2NJ

geniusmedia.pub   books@geniusmedia.pub

Loki is a velociraptor.

Velociraptors are hunters, they chase other dinosaurs.

Velociraptors are fast and clever. They work together in teams to solve problems and catch their food.

Velociraptors like to hunt in the jungle where they can hide behind the trees and bushes.

Loki is curious and smart and he loves to be busy, exploring and playing with his friends.

Loki likes to laugh and play tricks on his friends but he gets into trouble for having fun and not being serious.

Loki can run very fast when he goes off to explore but his Mum gets mad when he goes too far from home.

Loki is very curious but he gets told off for being nosey.

Loki enjoys going to school and learning about exciting new places to explore.

Loki loves to play tricks on his friends and making everyone laugh.

Loki likes school but he gets into trouble for having too much fun instead of paying attention to the teacher.

The teacher says that Loki won't learn anything if he keeps playing instead of studying.

Loki is sad because he keeps getting into trouble for doing all the things that he just loves to do. "I can't help it, I just love to have fun", he says.

His Mum wants him to be happy but she worries about him because she wants him to be safe too.

Loki's Mum wants him to be good at school so that he can learn lots of useful, interesting things that will help him in the future.

Loki's mum is off to have tea with her friends.

"You can play outside but don't go near the volcanoes!", she says.

She is worried that he might go too far from home, somewhere dangerous.

Loki doesn't understand why there are places he's not allowed to go.

"It's not fair", he thinks to himself. He doesn't understand, so he meets his friends and goes off to explore.

Loki doesn't know why his Mum thinks the volcanoes are dangerous, the area seems quiet and safe to play in.

It's the perfect place to run around and explore with his friends Thor and Freya.

There is lots of wide open space and so many interesting caves to nose around in.

Loki, Thor and Freya play together for hours and hours.

Suddenly, the ground starts to shake and clouds of thick dust shoot up into the air!

The volcanoes are starting to erupt!

As the sky turns red and black, Loki and his friends all run as fast as they can away from the volcanoes.

Thor and Freya run towards the jungle but Loki knows that the villagers are in danger. "I have to warn them!" he shouts.

Loki bravely runs to warn the villagers who quickly pick up their babies and run to safety – just in time!

The volcanoes are quiet again but the thick grey dust has settled on the village. It's time for everyone to clean up and make their homes neat and tidy again.

Loki's Mum is sad, "I lost my favourite necklace", she cries.

Loki makes himself busy and puts his talents to good use, exploring curiously.

Look at what he found in the dust!

Loki's special talents have turned out to be very important, after all.

Loki is such a good explorer that he takes the children in the village on exciting adventures in the jungle.

They all love to make new friends and discover new places that they only heard about at school.

All the Mummy dinosaurs know their babies are safe with Loki because he cares about them.

Loki loves to have fun and all the dinosaur babies love it when he plays with them.

Loki keeps them all entertained and he can always think of something new to do.

They play games all day long and Loki never gets bored or tired because he enjoys playing as much as they do!

Everyone in the village is so grateful to Loki for running to save them from the volcanoes.

If Loki had not gone to explore then he would not have discovered the volcanoes. Something terrible could have happened.

They make him his favourite snack as a 'thank you' and they all cheer Loki for saving the village.

"Hooray for Loki!" "Our hero!"

Everyone agrees that all the things that used to annoy them about Loki are really wonderful, valuable gifts and they love Loki even more, although...

He still likes to have fun and play tricks on his friends!

Loki and his friends learned an important lesson from their adventure. He says, "You're wonderful, just the way you are."

www.ingramcontent.com/pod-product-compliance
Lightning Source LLC
Chambersburg PA
CBHW041541040426
42446CB00002B/190